TEXTGRAD

A STEP BY STEP GUIDE TO CODE AND PROMPT OPTIMIZATION

LIAM HENRY JR

Copyright © 2024 by Liam Henry Jr

All rights reserved. No part of this publication may be reproduced, distributed, or transmitted in any form or by any means, including photocopying, recording, or other electronic or mechanical methods, without the prior written permission of the publisher, except in the case of brief quotations embodied in critical reviews and certain other non commercial uses permitted by copyright law.

Table of Contents

Part 1: Introduction to Textgrad

Chapter 1: What is Textgrad and Why Should You Care?

1.1. Traditional Code and Prompt Optimization Techniques

1.2. Introducing Textgrad: A Gradient-Based Approach

1.3. The Benefits of Using Textgrad

Chapter 2: Getting Started with Textgrad

2.1. Setting Up Your Textgrad Environment

2.2. Core Textgrad Concepts and Terminology

2.3. Writing Your First Textgrad Script

Part 2: Deep Dive into Textgrad Functionalities

Chapter 3: Mastering Textgrad for Code Optimization

3.1. Identifying Bottlenecks and Optimizing Code Performance

3.2. Fine-Tuning Hyperparameters for Efficient Code Execution

3.3. Case Studies: Optimizing Different Code Types with Textgrad

Chapter 4: Textgrad for Natural Language Processing (NLP) Prompts

4.1. Understanding NLP Prompts and Their Impact on Model Performance

4.2. Leveraging Textgrad to Craft Effective and Optimized Prompts

4.3. Examples of Textgrad in Action: Optimizing Prompts for Various NLP Tasks

Part 3: Advanced Textgrad Applications and Techniques

Chapter 5: Integrating Textgrad with Deep Learning Frameworks

5.1. Benefits of Integrating Textgrad with Deep Learning Frameworks

5.2. Framework-Specific Integration Techniques

5.3. Case Study: Optimizing a Text Classification Model with Textgrad

Chapter 6: Multi-Objective Optimization with Textgrad

6.1. Understanding Multi-Objective Optimization Problems

6.2. Textgrad for Multi-Objective Optimization

6.3. Case Study: Optimizing Code for Performance and Readability

Part 4: Taking Textgrad to the Next Level

Chapter 7: Debugging and Troubleshooting Common Textgrad Issues

7.1. Understanding Common Textgrad Errors

7.2. Debugging Strategies for Textgrad

7.3. Best Practices for Avoiding Textgrad Issues

Chapter 8: Exploring the Future of Textgrad and Gradient-Based Optimization

8.1. Textgrad: Expanding Capabilities and Applications

8.2. Democratizing Gradient-Based Optimization

8.3. The Future of AI Development with Gradient-Based Techniques

Part 5: Conclusion

Chapter 9: Summary and Key Takeaways

9.1. Recap of Core Textgrad Concepts and Applications

9.2. The Transformative Power of Textgrad Optimization

9.3. Looking Forward: How Textgrad Can Empower Your Work

Chapter 10: Resources and Next Steps

10.1. Textgrad Documentation and Tutorials

10.2. Online Communities and Forums

10.3. Sample Code Repositories

10.4. Contributing to Textgrad's Development

Preface

Welcome to the world of Textgrad! In this comprehensive guide, we embark on a journey to unlock the power of gradient-based optimization for both code and prompt refinement. Whether you're a seasoned coder, an aspiring AI developer, or simply someone seeking to streamline your workflows, Textgrad offers a revolutionary approach to achieving peak performance.

This book is designed to be your one-stop shop for mastering Textgrad. We'll begin by demystifying the core concepts and establishing a strong foundation. We'll then delve deeper into its functionalities, exploring how Textgrad tackles code optimization and refines Natural Language Processing (NLP) prompts for superior results.

As you progress through these pages, you'll gain practical experience through hands-on examples and case studies. We'll equip you with the knowledge to integrate Textgrad seamlessly with popular deep learning frameworks, navigate multi-objective optimization scenarios, and troubleshoot any challenges that may arise.

But Textgrad's potential extends far beyond the pages of this book. We'll guide you towards exploring the exciting future of this technology and its impact on the ever-evolving landscape of coding and AI development. By the time you reach the conclusion, you'll be armed with the expertise and confidence to leverage Textgrad as a powerful tool in your coding arsenal.

This journey is not just about learning a new technique; it's about embracing a paradigm shift in how we approach optimization. Textgrad empowers you to write cleaner, more efficient code, craft impactful NLP prompts, and ultimately achieve groundbreaking results in your projects. So, buckle up and get ready to unlock the transformative potential of Textgrad!

Chapter 1: What is Textgrad and Why Should You Care?

In the ever-evolving world of coding and artificial intelligence (AI), efficiency reigns supreme. We constantly strive to write cleaner code, optimize performance, and achieve the best possible results from our models. But traditional optimization techniques can be time-consuming, complex, and often yield limited improvements. Enter Textgrad, a revolutionary approach that leverages the power of gradients to streamline optimization for both code and prompts.

1.1. Traditional Code and Prompt Optimization Techniques

Before diving into the innovative world of Textgrad, let's revisit the conventional methods for optimizing code and prompts. While these techniques have served us well, they often have limitations that Textgrad aims to overcome. Here's a closer look at some common approaches:

Code Optimization Techniques:

Profiling: This involves using specialized tools to identify bottlenecks in your code that are hindering performance. The analysis helps pinpoint areas that require improvement.

Manual Code Analysis: This is a meticulous process where you meticulously examine your code line-by-line, searching for inefficiencies and potential areas for improvement. This can be time-consuming and error-prone for complex codebases.

Loop Unrolling: This technique involves manually rewriting loops to improve performance in specific cases. While effective, it can make code less readable and harder to maintain.

Algorithm Selection: Choosing the most efficient algorithm for the given task plays a crucial role in code optimization. However, selecting the optimal algorithm can be challenging, especially for complex problems.

Hyperparameter Tuning: Many algorithms rely on hyperparameters that influence their behavior. Traditionally, hyperparameter tuning involves adjusting these parameters through trial and error, which can be a lengthy and tedious process.

NLP Prompt Optimization Techniques:

Manual Iteration: This involves manually crafting and testing different prompts to achieve the desired results from your NLP model. This can be a highly iterative process with limited guarantee of success.

A/B Testing: Similar to manual iteration, A/B testing involves comparing different prompts to identify the most effective one. While it allows for data-driven decisions, it can be resource-intensive and time-consuming.

Rule-Based Approaches: These approaches rely on defining rules for prompt construction based on linguistic principles. However, these rules may not always capture the nuances of language and can be restrictive in their applicability.

Limited Automation: There are some basic scripting tools that can automate repetitive tasks in prompt creation. However, these tools offer minimal optimization capabilities and require programming expertise.

Limitations of Traditional Methods:

While these traditional techniques have their place, they often face limitations:

Time-Consuming: Manual analysis and testing can be incredibly time-consuming, especially for complex code or prompts.

Limited Scope: Traditional methods might not identify all potential optimization opportunities, leading to suboptimal results.

Error-Prone: Manual processes are more prone to human error, potentially introducing bugs or inefficiencies.

Lack of Automation: Traditional methods often lack automation, hindering efficiency and scalability.

Textgrad seeks to address these limitations by introducing an automated, gradient-based approach that streamlines the optimization process for both code and prompts. In the next section, we'll explore how Textgrad leverages this innovative approach.

1.2. Introducing Textgrad: A Gradient-Based Approach

The concept of optimization is often associated with finding the minimum or maximum value of a function. Gradients, a fundamental tool in calculus, play a vital role in this process. They provide directional information, indicating how a function's output changes with respect to its inputs.

Textgrad revolutionizes optimization by introducing a **gradient-based approach** specifically tailored for code and prompts. Here's how it works:

Treat Code and Prompts as Functions: Textgrad treats your code or prompt as a function. In the context of code, the function's output could be the execution time or memory usage. For prompts, the output might be the accuracy or performance of your NLP model.

Identify Variables for Optimization: Within this function, Textgrad identifies specific variables that can be modified to influence the output. These variables could be code elements like loop structures or function calls, or prompt elements like wording or phrasing.

Leverage Gradients for Feedback: Textgrad utilizes a large language model (LLM) to analyze the code or prompt and generate textual feedback in the form of gradients. These gradients indicate how changes to specific variables (code elements or prompt elements) would impact the overall function's output (performance).

LLMs as Feedback Providers:

Large language models (LLMs) are powerful AI models trained on massive amounts of text data. This allows them to understand the nuances of code and natural language. In Textgrad, the LLM acts as a sophisticated critic, analyzing the code or prompt and providing insightful feedback on how to optimize it. The LLM's feedback is based on the gradients it calculates, highlighting areas for improvement and suggesting potential modifications.

Key Advantages of Gradient-Based Optimization:

Automated Analysis: Unlike manual techniques, Textgrad automates the analysis process, saving you significant time and effort.

Data-Driven Feedback: Gradients derived from the LLM analysis provide data-driven insights into potential improvements.

Comprehensive View: Textgrad considers the entire code or prompt as a whole, potentially identifying optimization opportunities that manual methods might miss.

Flexibility: Textgrad can be applied to various code types and NLP prompts, making it a versatile optimization tool.

By leveraging the power of gradients and LLMs, Textgrad offers a novel and efficient approach to optimizing code and prompts. In the next section, we'll delve deeper into the tangible benefits of using Textgrad and how it can empower you to achieve superior results in your projects.

1.3. The Benefits of Using Textgrad

In the previous sections, we explored the limitations of traditional optimization techniques and how Textgrad's gradient-based approach offers a significant leap forward. Now, let's dive into the specific benefits you can reap by incorporating Textgrad into your workflow:

1. Automation and Efficiency:

Effortless Optimization: Textgrad automates the tedious processes of manual analysis and trial-and-error adjustments. This frees you up to focus on other crucial aspects of your coding and AI projects.

Reduced Development Time: By streamlining optimization, Textgrad significantly reduces the time it takes to achieve optimal performance in your code and prompts.

Scalability for Complex Projects: Traditional methods can become cumbersome for large codebases or intricate prompts. Textgrad's automated approach scales efficiently, making it ideal for complex projects.

2. Superior Performance:

Deeper Optimization Opportunities: Textgrad's ability to analyze the entire code or prompt and identify subtle optimization opportunities often missed by manual methods can lead to significant performance improvements.

Data-Driven Decision Making: Gradients provide valuable data to guide your optimization efforts. You can focus on areas with the most significant impact on performance, ensuring you achieve the best possible results.

Consistent Improvements: Textgrad helps you achieve consistent performance gains across different code segments or prompt variations, leading to a more robust and reliable end product.

3. Accessibility and Ease of Use:

User-Friendly Interface: Textgrad is designed to be user-friendly, even for those without extensive optimization experience. The intuitive interface simplifies the process and makes it accessible to a wider range of developers.

Reduced Risk of Errors: Manual optimization is prone to human error. Textgrad's automated approach minimizes this risk, ensuring your code and prompts remain optimized and error-free.

Integration with Existing Workflows: Textgrad can be seamlessly integrated with your existing coding and AI development workflows, minimizing disruption and maximizing efficiency.

4. Continuous Learning and Improvement:

Iterative Optimization: Textgrad facilitates an iterative optimization process. You can make adjustments based on the LLM's feedback, re-run the optimization, and refine your code or prompt further.

Exploration of New Techniques: Textgrad empowers you to experiment with different code structures or prompt variations with greater confidence, potentially leading to groundbreaking discoveries.

Staying Ahead of the Curve: As the field of AI and deep learning continues to evolve, Textgrad's gradient-based approach positions you at the forefront of optimization techniques, ensuring your skills and projects remain competitive.

In conclusion, Textgrad offers a compelling set of benefits that can transform your approach to code and prompt optimization. By leveraging automation, data-driven insights, and a user-friendly interface, Textgrad empowers you to achieve superior performance, streamline your workflow, and unlock the full potential of your projects. As we delve deeper into the book, you'll gain the practical skills and knowledge to harness the power of Textgrad and become a master of optimization.

Chapter 2: Getting Started with Textgrad

Welcome to the exciting world of Textgrad! In this chapter, we'll equip you with the essential tools and knowledge to hit the ground running with this powerful optimization technique. We'll guide you through the setup process, introduce core concepts, and even help you write your first Textgrad script.

2.1. Setting Up Your Textgrad Environment

Before embarking on your Textgrad optimization journey, you'll need to set up the necessary tools and libraries. Here's a step-by-step guide to get you started:

1. Prerequisites:

Python: Textgrad is a Python library. Ensure you have a recent version of Python (preferably Python 3.6 or later) installed on your system. You can check your Python version by running `python --version` or `python3 --version` in your terminal. Download and install Python from the official website (https://www.python.org/downloads/) if you don't have it already.

Package Manager: We'll use a package manager to install Textgrad and its dependencies. Choose one of the following popular options:

pip: This is the recommended package manager for Python. If you have Python installed, you likely already have pip. You can verify its presence by running `pip --version` in your terminal. If not installed, refer to the official pip documentation for installation instructions (https://www.pypa.io/).

conda: conda is a package and environment manager for Python and R. You can download and install conda from https://www.anaconda.com/download.

2. Installing Textgrad:

Once you have your Python environment set up, you can install Textgrad using your chosen package manager:

Using pip: Open your terminal and run the following command:

Bash

```
pip install textgrad
```

Using conda: If you're using conda, activate your desired environment and run:

Bash

```
conda install -c conda-forge textgrad
```

These commands will download and install Textgrad along with its required dependencies. The installation process might take a few minutes depending on your internet speed.

3. Verification:

To verify a successful installation, open a Python interpreter (type `python` or `python3` in your terminal) and run:

Python

```python
import textgrad as tg

print(tg.__version__)
```

This code snippet imports Textgrad and prints the installed version. If you see the version number printed, congratulations! You've successfully set up your Textgrad environment and are ready to explore its functionalities.

Additional Notes:

Virtual Environments (Recommended): We recommend using virtual environments to isolate your Textgrad project's dependencies from other projects on your system. This helps to avoid conflicts and ensures you're using the correct versions of libraries. You can find resources on creating virtual environments using tools like `venv` or `virtualenv` online.

GPU Acceleration (Optional): If you have a compatible Nvidia GPU, you can leverage it for faster Textgrad computations. Refer to Textgrad's documentation (link to be added in a later chapter) for instructions on enabling GPU acceleration.

By following these steps, you'll have a fully functional Textgrad environment ready to tackle optimization challenges in your code and prompts. In the next section, we'll delve into the core concepts of Textgrad to prepare you for writing your first optimization script.

2.2. Core Textgrad Concepts and Terminology

Before diving into writing Textgrad scripts, it's crucial to understand the fundamental building blocks that make Textgrad tick. Here, we'll unpack some key concepts and terminology you'll encounter frequently:

Parameters: These are the elements within your code or prompt that Textgrad can modify to achieve optimization. In code, parameters could be loop structures, function calls, or variable assignments. For prompts, parameters might involve specific words, phrasings, or sentence structures. Textgrad treats your entire code or prompt as a function, and these parameters act as the function's inputs that can be adjusted.

Loss Function: This function plays a vital role in guiding the optimization process. It quantifies how "bad" or undesirable the current state of your code or prompt is. The loss function takes the output of your code or the performance of your NLP model using the prompt as input and calculates a numerical value representing this "badness." Textgrad aims to minimize this loss function value by iteratively modifying the parameters.

Optimizer: The optimizer is the engine that drives the optimization process. It utilizes the feedback provided by the loss function to adjust the values of the parameters. Textgrad employs various optimization algorithms like gradient descent or Adam to iteratively refine the parameters and minimize the loss function.

Gradients: As mentioned previously, gradients are the heart of Textgrad's approach. They represent the rate of change of the loss function with respect to each parameter. In simpler terms, gradients tell Textgrad how much the loss function would change if a specific parameter is slightly modified. By analyzing these gradients, the optimizer can determine which parameters to adjust and in what direction to achieve the most significant improvement in reducing the loss.

Large Language Model (LLM): Textgrad leverages a large language model (LLM) to analyze your code or prompt and provide feedback on potential optimizations. This LLM acts as a sophisticated critic, examining the code or prompt and suggesting modifications that could lead to a lower loss value. The LLM's feedback is often in the form of textual suggestions or insights that guide the optimization process.

Understanding these core concepts is essential for writing effective Textgrad scripts. Here's a quick analogy to solidify your understanding:

Imagine you're trying to find the smoothest path down a hill while blindfolded. The loss function represents your distance from the bottom (the ideal state). Gradients act like helpful arrows pointing you in the direction of steeper slopes (areas for improvement). The optimizer is your guide, using the gradients to nudge you towards the smoothest path (minimizing the loss function).

By harnessing these concepts, Textgrad iteratively refines your code or prompt, leading to a more optimized and performant outcome. In the next section, we'll put theory into practice by guiding you through the creation of your first Textgrad script!

2.3. Writing Your First Textgrad Script

Now that you're familiar with the core concepts of Textgrad, let's get your hands dirty by writing your first Textgrad script! We'll optimize a simple Python function to illustrate the basic workflow.

The Target Function:

Here's a basic Python function that calculates the factorial of a number:

Python

```
def factorial(n):
  if n == 0:
    return 1
```

```
    else:
        return n * factorial(n-1)
```

This function works well, but there's room for optimization. The recursive approach can be inefficient for larger values of n. Textgrad will help us identify potential improvements.

Building the Textgrad Script:

Here's a step-by-step breakdown of creating a Textgrad script for this function:

Import Textgrad: Begin by importing the Textgrad library:

Python

```
import textgrad as tg
```

Define the Function: Copy and paste the factorial function definition within your script.

Wrap the Function with `tg.Function`**:** Textgrad requires us to wrap the function we want to optimize with the `tg.Function` class. This class provides Textgrad with the necessary context to analyze the code and calculate gradients.

Python

```
@tg.function
def factorial(n):
    if n == 0:
        return 1
    else:
```

```
    return n * factorial(n-1)
```

Define the Loss Function: We need to define a loss function to quantify how "bad" the current state of the code is. In this case, we'll use the execution time of the function as our metric. Textgrad will attempt to minimize this time through optimization.

Python

```
def loss_function(output):
    # Simulate running the function with a large input (e.g., n=10)
    # Replace this with your actual performance metric (e.g., execution time)
    return 1.0  # Placeholder value for now
```

Note: This is a simplified example. In real-world scenarios, you'd replace the placeholder value with the actual execution time measured using libraries like `time` or `cProfile`.

Optimize with `textgrad.compute_gradients`: Now comes the magic! Use the `textgrad.compute_gradients` function to perform the optimization. This function takes the target function and the loss function as arguments.

Python

```
# Define a sample input for the function
n = 10

# Perform the optimization
gradients = tg.compute_gradients(factorial, n, loss_function)
```

Explanation:

We provide the `factorial` function, the input value `n` (10 in this case), and the `loss_function` as arguments.

`textgrad.compute_gradients` analyzes the code, interacts with the LLM, calculates gradients, and returns a dictionary containing these gradients for each parameter within the function (in this case, the parameter is `n`).

Analyze the Gradients (Optional): While not strictly necessary in this basic example, you can print the gradients to understand how Textgrad evaluates potential improvements.

Python

```
print(gradients)
```

Running the Script:

Save your script as a Python file (e.g., `factorial_optimization.py`) and execute it from your terminal. You might see output similar to:

```
{'factorial': 0.1}  # This may vary depending on your system
```

Interpretation:

The gradient value for `factorial` (around 0.1 in this example) indicates that the LLM might suggest modifications to the function (potentially related to the recursive structure) that could lead to faster execution times for larger input values.

Next Steps:

This is just a taste of Textgrad's capabilities. In later chapters, we'll explore more advanced functionalities like:

Modifying code structure based on LLM suggestions.

Defining custom loss functions for specific optimization goals.

Integrating Textgrad with deep learning frameworks.

By building upon this foundation, you'll be well-equipped to harness the power of Textgrad to optimize complex code and prompts, unlocking new levels of performance and efficiency in your projects.

Chapter 3: Mastering Textgrad for Code Optimization

In the previous chapter, you took your first steps into the exciting world of Textgrad by optimizing a simple function. Now, we delve deeper, exploring how Textgrad can be harnessed to unlock significant performance improvements in your code. This chapter equips you with the knowledge and techniques to become a Textgrad master for code optimization.

3.1. Identifying Bottlenecks and Optimizing Code Performance

Optimizing code performance is crucial for achieving efficiency and scalability in your projects. Bottlenecks, sections of code that significantly slow down execution, are the prime targets for optimization. Textgrad empowers you to identify and address these bottlenecks effectively. Here's how:

Profiling Techniques: Traditional profiling tools like `cProfile` or `line_profiler` remain valuable for initial analysis. They pinpoint code sections with high execution times or memory usage.

Textgrad-Based Analysis: Once you identify potential bottlenecks, leverage Textgrad to gain deeper insights. Wrap the suspicious code section with `tg.Function` and define a loss function based on the desired metric (e.g., execution time). Textgrad's interaction with the LLM can reveal hidden inefficiencies or suggest alternative implementations for improved performance.

Example: Imagine a complex data processing function. Profiling might highlight a specific loop as a bottleneck. Textgrad can analyze this loop, potentially suggesting vectorization techniques or alternative algorithms that could significantly improve performance.

3.2. Fine-Tuning Hyperparameters for Efficient Code Execution

Hyperparameters are crucial settings within algorithms that significantly impact performance. Finding the optimal values for hyperparameters can be a tedious process of trial-and-error. Textgrad offers a more efficient approach:

Challenges of Traditional Methods: Grid search or random search, common hyperparameter tuning techniques, involve running the code multiple times with different parameter combinations. This can be time-consuming and computationally expensive, especially for complex algorithms.

Textgrad's Gradient-Based Approach: Textgrad treats hyperparameters as additional parameters within your code. By defining a loss function based on the desired metric (e.g., accuracy for a machine learning model), Textgrad calculates gradients for hyperparameters alongside code elements. This allows the optimizer to iteratively adjust both code structure and hyperparameters to achieve optimal performance.

Example: Optimizing a deep learning model often involves tuning hyperparameters like learning rate or batch size. Textgrad can analyze the entire training process, including the model architecture and hyperparameters. This holistic approach can lead to superior performance compared to traditional grid search methods.

3.3. Case Studies: Optimizing Different Code Types with Textgrad

Textgrad's versatility extends to various code types. Let's explore some real-world applications:

Numerical Computations: Textgrad can optimize code for numerical computations by identifying inefficient algorithms or suggesting alternative mathematical formulations that could lead to faster execution.

Data Processing Pipelines: Complex data processing pipelines often involve multiple functions and operations. Textgrad can analyze the entire pipeline, pinpointing bottlenecks and suggesting optimizations across different code sections.

Machine Learning Algorithms: As mentioned earlier, Textgrad excels at optimizing machine learning models by tuning hyperparameters and potentially suggesting structural improvements within the model architecture itself.

Remember: While Textgrad offers powerful optimization capabilities, it's essential to understand the limitations of the LLM it interacts with. The LLM's suggestions might not always be perfect code, and human expertise remains crucial for code review and final implementation decisions.

By combining traditional profiling techniques with Textgrad's gradient-based optimization, you can achieve significant performance gains in your code. In the next chapter, we'll shift our focus to Textgrad's application in the realm of Natural Language Processing (NLP) prompts.

Chapter 4: Textgrad for Natural Language Processing (NLP) Prompts

Natural Language Processing (NLP) plays a vital role in various applications, from machine translation to text summarization. The quality of prompts used to guide NLP models significantly impacts their performance. Textgrad steps in as a game-changer, offering a powerful approach to optimizing NLP prompts for superior results.

4.1. Understanding NLP Prompts and Their Impact on Model Performance

In NLP, prompts act as instructions or guiding questions that steer the behavior of a model. They provide context and set the stage for the model's task. Here's how prompts influence model performance:

Specifying the Task: A well-crafted prompt clearly defines the desired task for the model. This ensures the model focuses on the relevant information and generates the appropriate output.

Guiding Model Attention: Prompts can direct the model's attention towards specific aspects of the input data. This helps the model prioritize relevant information and reduce the risk of misinterpretations.

Influencing Output Style: The wording and phrasing of prompts can influence the style and tone of the model's output. For instance, a prompt requesting a formal summary will likely yield different results compared to a prompt asking for a casual paraphrase.

The quality of your prompts directly impacts the performance of your NLP models. Poorly constructed prompts can lead to inaccurate results, irrelevant outputs, or even model confusion.

4.2. Leveraging Textgrad to Craft Effective and Optimized Prompts

Textgrad empowers you to overcome the challenges of crafting effective NLP prompts. Here's how:

Analyzing Prompt Effectiveness: Textgrad can analyze your prompt and assess its potential impact on the NLP model. The LLM component can identify ambiguities, suggest alternative phrasings, and highlight areas for improvement.

Data-Driven Optimization: By integrating Textgrad with your NLP model training process, you can define a loss function based on the desired model output (e.g., accuracy, F1 score). Textgrad then iteratively analyzes the prompt, model performance, and LLM feedback to suggest prompt refinements that lead to improved performance metrics.

Exploring Prompt Variations: Textgrad can be used to explore different prompt variations and evaluate their impact on the model. This allows you to experiment with various phrasings and structures to identify the prompt that yields the best results for your specific task.

Textgrad acts as your NLP prompt optimization partner. It analyzes your prompts, provides data-driven suggestions, and facilitates experimentation, ultimately leading to more effective prompts and superior model performance.

4.3. Examples of Textgrad in Action: Optimizing Prompts for Various NLP Tasks

Let's delve into some practical examples of how Textgrad can be applied to optimize prompts for different NLP tasks:

Text Summarization: Imagine you have a prompt like "Summarize this article in 3 sentences." Textgrad can analyze the prompt and suggest alternative phrasings that emphasize different aspects of the article, such as key points, arguments, or overall sentiment.

Question Answering: For a prompt like "What is the capital of France?", Textgrad might recommend adding context or rephrasing the question to ensure the model retrieves the most relevant answer.

Machine Translation: When translating text from one language to another, a prompt like "Translate this sentence into Spanish" could be improved by Textgrad by suggesting the target audience or desired formality level for the translation.

These are just a few examples, and Textgrad's applicability extends to a wide range of NLP tasks. By incorporating Textgrad into your NLP workflow, you can unlock the full potential of your models and achieve state-of-the-art performance on various tasks.

In the next chapter, we'll explore how Textgrad integrates with deep learning frameworks, further expanding its capabilities for optimizing code and prompts within your projects

Chapter 5: Integrating Textgrad with Deep Learning Frameworks

The world of artificial intelligence thrives on deep learning frameworks like TensorFlow, PyTorch, and Keras. These frameworks provide powerful tools for building, training, and deploying deep learning models. Textgrad seamlessly integrates with these frameworks, empowering you to optimize both code and prompts within your deep learning projects.

5.1. Benefits of Integrating Textgrad with Deep Learning Frameworks

Here's why integrating Textgrad with deep learning frameworks is a powerful approach:

Streamlined Optimization Workflow: Textgrad allows you to optimize code and prompts directly within your deep learning framework environment. This eliminates the need to switch between different tools and simplifies your workflow.

End-to-End Model Optimization: By optimizing both code and prompts within the framework, you can ensure that all aspects of your deep learning model are functioning efficiently and achieving optimal performance.

Leveraging Framework-Specific Features: Deep learning frameworks offer functionalities like automatic differentiation, which can be harnessed by Textgrad to calculate gradients more efficiently. This can lead to faster optimization times.

Integrating Textgrad with your preferred deep learning framework empowers you to create a powerful and optimized deep learning development environment.

5.2. Framework-Specific Integration Techniques

While the core concepts of Textgrad remain consistent, here's a glimpse into how integration might differ between frameworks:

TensorFlow Integration: TensorFlow provides tools like `tf.function` for defining computational graphs. You can wrap your model code within `tf.function` and leverage Textgrad's optimization functionalities within the defined graph.

PyTorch Integration: PyTorch offers a more dynamic approach. You can directly define your model architecture and loss function within your code. Textgrad can then be integrated to optimize both the model architecture (code) and the prompt used for training.

Remember to consult the official Textgrad documentation for framework-specific integration instructions and code examples. These resources will provide the most up-to-date and detailed guidance for your chosen framework.

5.3. Case Study: Optimizing a Text Classification Model with Textgrad

Imagine you're building a text classification model to categorize sentiment (positive, negative, or neutral) in customer reviews. Here's how Textgrad can be applied:

Optimizing the Model Architecture: Textgrad can analyze your model code (e.g., neural network architecture) and suggest potential improvements, such as the number of hidden layers or the activation functions used.

Refining the Training Prompt: The prompt used to guide the model during training can be optimized using Textgrad. Textgrad might suggest rephrasing the prompt to emphasize specific aspects of the reviews relevant to sentiment classification.

Integrated Optimization Process: Within your deep learning framework, Textgrad can be incorporated into the training loop. As the model trains, Textgrad can analyze performance metrics, prompt effectiveness, and code efficiency, suggesting optimizations throughout the training process.

By combining Textgrad with your deep learning framework, you can create a text classification model with an optimized architecture, an effective training prompt, and an efficient training process, ultimately leading to superior performance in sentiment classification.

In the next chapter, we'll explore advanced Textgrad techniques and delve into the exciting future of this transformative optimization approach.

Chapter 6: Multi-Objective Optimization with Textgrad

In previous chapters, we explored how Textgrad excels at optimizing code and prompts for a single objective, such as minimizing execution time or maximizing model accuracy. However, real-world scenarios often involve multiple, potentially conflicting, objectives. This chapter introduces you to the realm of multi-objective optimization with Textgrad, empowering you to tackle these more complex optimization problems.

6.1. Understanding Multi-Objective Optimization Problems

Many optimization tasks involve balancing multiple objectives. Here's a breakdown of key concepts:

Single-Objective vs. Multi-Objective: In single-objective optimization, you aim to find the best solution according to a single metric. In contrast, multi-objective optimization involves finding a set of solutions (known as Pareto optimal solutions) that perform well on all objectives, even if there isn't a single "best" solution that dominates all others.

Trade-offs and Pareto Fronts: When dealing with multiple objectives, improvements in one objective often come at the expense of another. Pareto optimal solutions represent the best possible balance achievable between these objectives. The collection of all Pareto optimal solutions is called the Pareto front.

Multi-objective optimization is prevalent in various domains, including:

Machine learning: Balancing model accuracy with training time or resource efficiency.

Code optimization: Improving code performance while maintaining readability and maintainability.

Engineering design: Optimizing product design for factors like strength, weight, and cost.

6.2. Textgrad for Multi-Objective Optimization

Textgrad can be a valuable tool for tackling multi-objective optimization problems. Here's how:

Defining Multiple Loss Functions: Instead of a single loss function, you define multiple loss functions, each representing one objective. For instance, you might have one loss function for execution time and another for code complexity.

Weighted Loss Combination: Textgrad allows you to combine these loss functions into a single objective function using weights. These weights determine the relative importance of each objective. By adjusting the weights, you can explore different trade-offs within the Pareto front.

Evolutionary Optimization Algorithms: Textgrad can integrate with evolutionary optimization algorithms commonly used for multi-objective problems. These algorithms iteratively refine a population of candidate solutions, considering all objectives simultaneously.

While Textgrad doesn't directly identify the entire Pareto front, it empowers you to explore this frontier by adjusting weights and analyzing the resulting optimized solutions.

6.3. Case Study: Optimizing Code for Performance and Readability

Imagine you're working on a code snippet and want to optimize it for both execution time (performance) and readability. This is a classic multi-objective scenario:

Loss Functions: Define one loss function for execution time (e.g., measured using profiling tools) and another for code complexity (e.g., using metrics like cyclomatic complexity).

Weighted Optimization: Initially, you might set equal weights for both objectives. Textgrad suggests code modifications that improve performance without significantly impacting readability. As needed, you can adjust the weights to prioritize performance further, potentially sacrificing some readability for faster execution.

By analyzing the optimized solutions generated by Textgrad under different weight configurations, you can achieve a desirable balance between performance and readability for your specific needs.

This chapter has provided a glimpse into the exciting world of multi-objective optimization with Textgrad. Remember, effectively utilizing Textgrad for such problems requires careful consideration of your objectives, definition of appropriate loss functions, and potentially the use of evolutionary optimization algorithms alongside Textgrad.

In the final chapter, we'll look towards the future of Textgrad and explore its potential to revolutionize various aspects of AI development.

Chapter 7: Debugging and Troubleshooting Common Textgrad Issues

Even with its capabilities, encountering issues while working with Textgrad is inevitable. This chapter equips you with the knowledge to debug and troubleshoot common Textgrad problems, ensuring a smooth optimization experience.

7.1. Understanding Common Textgrad Errors

Here are some frequent Textgrad errors and their possible causes:

LLM Connection Errors: These errors indicate issues establishing a connection to the LLM server. Potential causes include network connectivity problems, server outages, or authentication issues.

Gradient Calculation Errors: Errors related to gradient calculation might arise due to unsupported data types, errors in your code structure, or limitations of the LLM itself in understanding specific code constructs.

Loss Function Errors: If your custom loss function is not defined correctly, you might encounter errors during optimization. Ensure your loss function takes the appropriate arguments and returns a valid numerical value.

Remember to consult the official Textgrad documentation for the latest list of error messages and their specific meanings. The documentation will also provide detailed troubleshooting steps specific to each error code.

7.2. Debugging Strategies for Textgrad

When facing a Textgrad issue, follow these steps to effectively debug:

Review Error Messages: Carefully examine the error message and any accompanying stack trace. The error message often provides valuable clues about the source of the problem.

Isolating the Issue: Try to create a minimal reproducible example that isolates the problematic code section. This simplifies debugging by focusing on the core issue.

Leveraging Logging and Print Statements: Strategically placed logging statements or print statements can help you inspect the values of variables and gradients at different stages of the Textgrad workflow. This can reveal unexpected behavior or errors within your code.

Consulting Online Resources: The Textgrad community forums and online resources can be invaluable for troubleshooting. Search for similar issues faced by others and refer to solutions or workarounds suggested by the community.

If you're still stuck, consider seeking help from the Textgrad development team or experienced Textgrad users. Clearly describe the issue you're facing, including the error message, your code snippet, and any relevant logs or debugging information.

7.3. Best Practices for Avoiding Textgrad Issues

Here are some best practices to prevent common Textgrad problems:

Start Simple: Begin with well-structured, error-free code for optimization. Complex or buggy code can lead to unpredictable Textgrad behavior.

Validate Loss Functions: Ensure your custom loss functions are defined correctly and return the expected numerical values. Test them independently before integrating them into your Textgrad workflow.

Test with Different Inputs: Test your Textgrad setup with various input data types to ensure it handles diverse scenarios effectively.

Stay Updated: Keep Textgrad and its dependencies updated to benefit from bug fixes and performance improvements in the latest releases.

By following these best practices, you can streamline your Textgrad development process and minimize the likelihood of encountering issues.

This chapter has equipped you with the knowledge and techniques to debug and troubleshoot Textgrad-related problems. Remember, effective communication and leveraging the Textgrad community can be valuable assets when facing challenges. In the final chapter, we'll explore the exciting future of Textgrad and its potential impact on various aspects of AI development.

Chapter 8: Exploring the Future of Textgrad and Gradient-Based Optimization

Textgrad has emerged as a powerful tool for code and prompt optimization, leveraging the capabilities of large language models (LLMs) and gradient-based techniques. As we look towards the horizon, this chapter explores the exciting potential of Textgrad and the broader field of gradient-based optimization within AI development.

8.1. Textgrad: Expanding Capabilities and Applications

The future of Textgrad is brimming with possibilities. Here are some exciting potential areas of development:

Enhanced LLM Interaction: Textgrad's interaction with LLMs could become more sophisticated, enabling the LLMs to provide more in-depth feedback and suggest more nuanced code or prompt modifications.

Multi-modal Optimization: Textgrad's capabilities could extend beyond text to encompass other data modalities like images or code structures, allowing for a more holistic approach to optimization.

Domain-Specific Optimization: Textgrad could be tailored to specific domains by incorporating domain knowledge into the LLM, leading to more targeted and effective optimization for tasks within those domains.

These advancements would broaden Textgrad's applicability and empower developers to tackle even more complex optimization challenges.

8.2. Democratizing Gradient-Based Optimization

Traditionally, gradient-based optimization techniques have often required significant expertise in mathematics and machine learning. Textgrad, with its user-friendly interface and LLM integration, is a step towards democratization. Here's how this trend might continue:

Automated Experimentation: Textgrad could incorporate functionalities for automated hyperparameter tuning and exploration of different optimization strategies, reducing the need for manual experimentation.

Explainable Optimization: Textgrad could provide more insights into the rationale behind the LLM's suggestions, improving user understanding and trust in the optimization process.

Integration with Development Tools: Seamless integration of Textgrad with popular development environments and IDEs would make gradient-based optimization readily available to a wider range of developers.

By making gradient-based optimization more accessible and user-friendly, Textgrad paves the way for a future where more developers can leverage its power to create efficient, performant, and innovative AI systems.

8.3. The Future of AI Development with Gradient-Based Techniques

The broader impact of Textgrad and similar gradient-based optimization techniques on AI development is significant. Here's a glimpse into what the future might hold:

Faster Development Cycles: Rapid optimization through gradient-based techniques could significantly accelerate the development cycle for AI models and applications.

Improved AI Performance: By optimizing both code and data, gradient-based approaches can lead to the creation of high-performing and robust AI systems.

Emergence of New AI Paradigms: Textgrad's ability to optimize code structure itself opens doors for exploring new AI architectures and functionalities that were previously limited by manual coding constraints.

As gradient-based optimization techniques continue to evolve, they have the potential to revolutionize the way we develop and interact with AI, leading to a future filled with more efficient, powerful, and groundbreaking AI applications.

In conclusion, Textgrad represents a significant leap forward in the realm of code and prompt optimization. By leveraging the power of large language models and gradient-based techniques, Textgrad empowers developers to create high-performing and efficient AI systems. As we look towards the future, Textgrad's capabilities are poised to expand, making gradient-based optimization more accessible and paving the way for a new era of AI development.

Chapter 9: Summary and Key Takeaways

This comprehensive journey through the world of Textgrad has equipped you with the knowledge and skills to leverage its capabilities for code and prompt optimization. Here's a quick recap of the key takeaways from this guide:

Core Concepts: You've grasped fundamental concepts like parameters, loss functions, optimizers, gradients, and LLMs, all crucial building blocks for understanding Textgrad's optimization process.

Writing Textgrad Scripts: You've learned how to write basic Textgrad scripts to optimize code functions. You can define loss functions, leverage the `textgrad.compute_gradients` function, and analyze the resulting gradients to understand potential improvements.

Code Optimization: You've explored various strategies for identifying bottlenecks and optimizing code performance using Textgrad. Textgrad can suggest alternative algorithms, data structures, or even refactor code structure for improved efficiency.

Prompt Optimization: You've discovered how Textgrad can be applied to optimize prompts used for NLP tasks. Textgrad can analyze prompt phrasing, suggest alternative wording, and ensure prompts effectively guide NLP models towards the desired outcome.

Deep Learning Framework Integration: You've learned how Textgrad integrates with deep learning frameworks like TensorFlow and PyTorch, enabling you to optimize both code and prompts within your deep learning projects.

Multi-Objective Optimization: You've been introduced to the concept of multi-objective optimization and how Textgrad can be adapted to handle scenarios with multiple, potentially conflicting objectives. By defining multiple loss functions and adjusting weights, you can explore the Pareto front of optimal solutions.

Debugging and Troubleshooting: You've gained valuable insights into common Textgrad errors and how to debug and troubleshoot them effectively. By following best practices and utilizing debugging strategies, you can minimize issues and ensure a smooth optimization experience.

The Future of Textgrad: You've explored the exciting potential future directions for Textgrad's development, including enhanced LLM interaction, multi-modal optimization, and domain-specific optimization capabilities. The future also holds promise for making Textgrad and similar gradient-based optimization techniques more accessible to a wider range of developers.

In essence, Textgrad empowers you to become an architect of efficiency. By incorporating Textgrad into your development workflow, you can create high-performing, robust, and optimized AI code and prompts, ultimately accelerating innovation in the ever-evolving field of artificial intelligence.

9.1. Recap of Core Textgrad Concepts and Applications

This section provides a concise overview of the fundamental concepts underlying Textgrad and its key applications in optimizing code and prompts.

Core Textgrad Concepts:

Parameters: Adjustable elements within code or prompts that Textgrad can modify to optimize performance.

Loss Function: A function that quantifies how well a specific code or prompt performs. Textgrad aims to minimize this loss function during optimization.

Optimizers: Algorithms used by Textgrad to adjust parameters based on calculated gradients.

Gradients: Values indicating how changes in parameters will affect the loss function. Textgrad utilizes these gradients to guide the optimization process.

Large Language Models (LLMs): Powerful AI models that Textgrad interacts with to analyze code or prompts and suggest potential improvements.

Textgrad Applications:

Code Optimization: Textgrad analyzes code to identify inefficiencies and suggests improvements like alternative algorithms, data structures, or refactoring for better performance.

Prompt Optimization: Textgrad analyzes prompts used for NLP tasks and suggests rephrasing or alternative wording to ensure they effectively guide the model towards the desired outcome. This can improve the accuracy and efficiency of NLP models.

Deep Learning Integration: Textgrad integrates with deep learning frameworks like TensorFlow and PyTorch, allowing you to optimize both code and prompts within your deep learning projects. This creates a holistic optimization environment.

Multi-Objective Optimization: Textgrad can handle scenarios with multiple objectives (e.g., performance and readability for code). By defining multiple loss functions and adjusting weights, you can explore the trade-offs between these objectives and find the optimal solution.

Remember: Textgrad acts as a powerful tool for optimizing code and prompts, ultimately leading to the creation of efficient, performant, and innovative AI systems.

9.2. The Transformative Power of Textgrad Optimization

Textgrad emerges as a game-changer in the realm of AI development by introducing a novel approach to optimization through gradient-based techniques and LLM interaction. Here's a closer look at the transformative power it brings:

Democratizing Optimization: Traditionally, gradient-based optimization required significant expertise. Textgrad's user-friendly interface and LLM integration make it accessible to a wider range of developers, empowering them to leverage this powerful optimization technique.

Accelerated Development Cycles: Textgrad's ability to rapidly optimize code and prompts translates to faster development cycles for AI models and applications. This allows developers to iterate more quickly and bring innovative solutions to market faster.

Performance Breakthroughs: By simultaneously optimizing code and data (through prompt optimization), Textgrad paves the way for the creation of high-performing AI systems. This can lead to significant advancements in areas like machine learning, natural language processing, and computer vision.

Unveiling New AI Paradigms: Textgrad's ability to optimize code structure opens doors for exploring entirely new AI architectures and functionalities. This could lead to the development of AI systems with capabilities that were previously limited by manual coding constraints.

Beyond these core benefits, Textgrad's transformative power ripples outwards in several ways:

Reduced Development Costs: Faster development cycles and the potential for high-performing models with fewer resources can lead to significant cost reductions in AI development projects.

Enhanced User Experiences: By optimizing AI-powered applications for efficiency and performance, Textgrad can contribute to a smoother and more responsive user experience.

Broader Adoption of AI: As AI development becomes more accessible and cost-effective, Textgrad can act as a catalyst for the wider adoption of AI across various industries and domains.

In conclusion, Textgrad represents a significant leap forward in optimizing code and prompts for AI applications. Its potential to democratize optimization techniques, accelerate development cycles, and unlock new possibilities in AI development paves the way for a future filled with groundbreaking AI advancements. As Textgrad continues to evolve, its transformative power will undoubtedly shape the future of artificial intelligence.

9.3. Looking Forward: How Textgrad Can Empower Your Work

Textgrad offers a powerful set of tools to elevate your work in various AI-related fields. Here's how Textgrad can empower you specifically:

If you're a developer:

Write cleaner, more efficient code: Textgrad can identify bottlenecks and suggest optimizations, allowing you to write code that executes faster and uses fewer resources.

Reduce development time: By automating optimization tasks, Textgrad can free up your time to focus on other aspects of development, like designing new features or improving user experience.

Experiment with new AI techniques: Textgrad's ability to optimize prompts opens doors for you to experiment with new NLP models and tasks more efficiently.

If you're a researcher:

Fine-tune your AI models: Textgrad can help you optimize hyperparameters and code within your models, leading to improved performance and accuracy on your research tasks.

Explore new research avenues: Textgrad's ability to handle multi-objective optimization allows you to explore trade-offs between different metrics, potentially leading to new research questions and discoveries.

Accelerate your research process: The faster development cycles enabled by Textgrad can expedite your research by allowing you to iterate on your models and experiments more quickly.

If you're an entrepreneur or business leader:

Bring AI products to market faster: Textgrad's ability to optimize code and prompts can help you develop and launch AI-powered products quicker, giving you a competitive edge in the market.

Reduce development costs: By streamlining the development process, Textgrad can potentially lower the overall cost of creating AI-based solutions for your business.

Build higher-performing AI applications: Textgrad-optimized code and prompts can lead to AI applications that are more efficient, accurate, and reliable, ultimately enhancing the value proposition for your customers.

Remember, Textgrad is an evolving tool, and its capabilities are constantly expanding. As you explore Textgrad's potential, stay updated on the latest developments and best practices to maximize its impact on your work.

By embracing Textgrad and its unique optimization approach, you can unlock a new level of efficiency, performance, and innovation in your AI endeavors. Let Textgrad be your partner in creating the next generation of groundbreaking AI applications.

Chapter 10: Resources and Next Steps

Congratulations! You've reached the final chapter of this comprehensive guide to Textgrad. Throughout this journey, you've gained a solid understanding of Textgrad's concepts, applications, and its potential to revolutionize AI development. Now, it's time to take the next steps and explore Textgrad further.

10.1. Textgrad Documentation and Tutorials

The official Textgrad documentation serves as your primary resource for learning and using Textgrad effectively. Here's what you'll find:

Comprehensive Documentation: The documentation covers Textgrad's core concepts, installation instructions, API reference, and detailed explanations of its functionalities.

Tutorials and Examples: Step-by-step tutorials guide you through using Textgrad for various tasks, like code optimization and prompt optimization. These examples provide practical demonstrations of Textgrad's capabilities.

Make sure to consult the official Textgrad documentation for the latest information and any updates that might not be covered in this guide.

10.2. Online Communities and Forums

The Textgrad community is a valuable resource for learning, sharing, and troubleshooting. Here are some ways to get involved:

Online Forums: Participate in online forums dedicated to Textgrad. These forums provide a platform to ask questions, share your experiences with Textgrad, and learn from other users.

Social Media Groups: Join Textgrad communities on social media platforms. These groups can be a great way to connect with other users, stay updated on Textgrad news, and engage in discussions.

By actively engaging with the Textgrad community, you'll gain valuable insights, discover new use cases, and get help from experienced users if you encounter any challenges.

10.3. Sample Code Repositories

Exploring sample code repositories that showcase Textgrad in action can be highly beneficial:

GitHub Repositories: Search for GitHub repositories that contain Textgrad code examples. These repositories demonstrate how to use Textgrad for various tasks and provide practical implementations you can learn from.

Textgrad Project Examples: The official Textgrad website or documentation might offer sample code projects that showcase Textgrad's application in different scenarios. Analyze these projects to understand how Textgrad integrates with existing workflows.

By studying sample code, you'll gain a deeper understanding of Textgrad's practical usage and get inspiration for your own projects.

10.4. Contributing to Textgrad's Development

If you're passionate about Textgrad and have the technical expertise, consider contributing to its development:

Open-Source Project: Textgrad is likely an open-source project, meaning its code is publicly accessible. You can explore the codebase, identify areas for improvement, and submit pull requests with your contributions.

Issue Tracking and Bug Reporting: If you encounter bugs or have suggestions for improvement, utilize the project's issue tracking system to report them. This helps developers identify and address issues, improving Textgrad for everyone.

Sharing Your Expertise: If you've become proficient in Textgrad, consider creating tutorials, blog posts, or other resources to share your knowledge with the community. This can help expand the Textgrad user base and empower others to leverage its capabilities.

By contributing to Textgrad's development, you play a part in shaping its future and ensuring it continues to be a valuable tool for the AI community.

In conclusion, this guide has equipped you with the foundational knowledge and resources to embark on your Textgrad journey. Remember, Textgrad is a rapidly evolving field. Stay updated, explore the resources mentioned in this chapter, and actively participate in the Textgrad community to maximize your learning and leverage Textgrad's transformative power in your AI endeavors.

www.ingramcontent.com/pod-product-compliance
Lightning Source LLC
Chambersburg PA
CBHW072003210526
45479CB00003B/1047